Q149 .U5 W5

Who was who in American
history–science and technology :...

DATE			

7698

Who Was Who in American History

Biographical Reference Works
Published by Marquis Who's Who, Inc.

Who's Who in America

Who's Who in America / Index by Professions

Who Was Who in America

   Historical Volume (1607-1896)

   Volume I (1897-1942)

   Volume II (1943-1950)

   Volume III (1951-1960)

   Volume IV (1961-1968)

   Volume V (1969-1973)

   Volume VI (1974-1976)

Who Was Who in American History — Arts and Letters

Who Was Who in American History — The Military

Who Was Who in American History — Science and Technology

Who's Who in the World

Who's Who in the East

Who's Who in the South and Southwest

Who's Who in the West

Who's Who in the Midwest

Who's Who of American Women

Who's Who in Religion

Who's Who in Finance and Industry

Who's Who in Government

Who's Who Biographical Record — Child Development Professionals

Who's Who Biographical Record — School District Officials

World Who's Who in Science

Directory of Medical Specialists

Directory of Osteopathic Specialists

International Scholars Directory

Marquis Who's Who Publications / Index to all Books